3/97

THE GREATEST AMERICAN SONGBOOK

W9-ACN-593

2	America (My Country, 'Tis Of Thee)
4	American Patrol
7	Anchors Aweigh
10	Army Air Corps Song (U.S. Air Force Song)
18	Battle Cry Of Freedom, The
20	Bell Bottom Trousers
22	Bonnie Blue Flag
24	Boys, Keep Your Powder Dry
15	Caisson Song, The (When The Caissons Go Rolling Along)
26	Columbia, The Gem Of The Ocean
34	Flag Song
36	God Bless Our Native Land
38	God Save America
40	Hail To The Chief
29	House I Live In, The
42	I Am An American (Shout! Wherever You May Be)
46	I Didn't Raise My Boy To Be A Soldier
51	Liberty Bell March
54	Liberty Song, The
56	Marine's Hymn
62	Onward Christian Soldiers
64	Our Flag Is There
66	Semper Fidelis
70	Stars And Stripes Forever
59	There's A Star Spangled Banner Waving Somewhere
76	Tramp, Tramp, Tramp
78	Washington Post March
84	We Are With You
82	Yankee Doodle

 Hal Leonard Publishing Corporation
7777 West Bluemound Road P.O. Box 13819 Milwaukee, WI 53213

ISBN 0-7935-0712-X

AMERICA
(MY COUNTRY, 'TIS OF THEE)

Additional Lyrics

3. Let music swell the breeze
   And ring from all the trees
   Sweet freedom's song.
   Let mortal tongues awake;
   Let all that breathe partake;
   Let rocks their silence break,
   The sound prolong.

4. Our fathers's God, to Thee
   Author of liberty,
   To Thee we sing.
   Long may our land be bright
   With freedom's holy light;
   Protect us by Thy might,
   Great God, our King!

AMERICAN PATROL

ANCHORS AWEIGH

ARMY AIR CORPS SONG
(U.S. AIR FORCE SONG)

By ROBERT CRAWFORD

THE CAISSON SONG
(WHEN THE CAISSONS GO ROLLING ALONG)

THE BATTLE CRY OF FREEDOM

Additional Lyrics

3. We will welcome to our numbers the loyal, true and brave,
Shouting the battle cry of freedom,
And although they may be poor not a man shall be a slave,
Shouting the battle cry of freedom.
(To Chorus:)

4. So we're springing to the call from the East and from the West,
Shouting the battle cry of freedom,
And we'll hurl the Rebel crew from the land we love the best,
Shouting the battle cry of freedom.
(To Chorus:)

BELL BOTTOM TROUSERS

Oh she was a la - dy's maid, I do not know her name. ____ Her mas - ter, he was kind to her; her mis - tress was the same. ____ A - long came a sail - or who

BONNIE BLUE FLAG

BOYS, KEEP YOUR POWDER DRY

COLUMBIA, THE GEM OF THE OCEAN

THE HOUSE I LIVE IN

Words by LEWIS ALLAN
Music by EARL ROBINSON

FLAG SONG

GOD BLESS OUR NATIVE LAND

GOD SAVE AMERICA

HAIL TO THE CHIEF

I AM AN AMERICAN
(SHOUT! WHEREVER YOU MAY BE)

Lyric and Music by IRA SCHUSTER,
PAUL CUNNINGHAM and LEONARD WHITCUP

I DIDN'T RAISE MY BOY TO BE A SOLDIER

Ten mil - lion sol - diers to the
What vic - tor - y can cheer a

war have gone who may nev - er re -
moth - er's heart when she looks at her

bles.   It's   time   to   lay   the   sword   and   gun   a-

way. _____   There'd   be   no   war   to - day   if

moth - ers   all   would   say,   "I   did - n't   raise   my

boy   to   be   a   sol -   dier."   "I   dier."

LIBERTY BELL MARCH

8va basso

THE LIBERTY SONG

MARINE'S HYMN

THERE'S A STAR SPANGLED BANNER WAVING SOMEWHERE

Words and Music by PAUL ROBERTS
and SHELBY DARNELL

ONWARD CHRISTIAN SOLDIERS

March tempo

On - ward, Chris - tian sol - diers march - ing as to
Like a might - y ar - my moves the church of
On - ward, then, ye peo - ple join our hap - py

war with the cross of Je - sus go - ing on be -
God. Broth - ers we are tread - ing where the saints have
throng. Blend with ours your voic - es in the tri - umph

fore! Christ, the roy - al Mas - ter, leads a - gainst the
trod. We are not di - vid - ed, all one bod - y
song. Glo - ry, laud, and hon - or un - to Christ the

OUR FLAG IS THERE

SEMPER FIDELIS

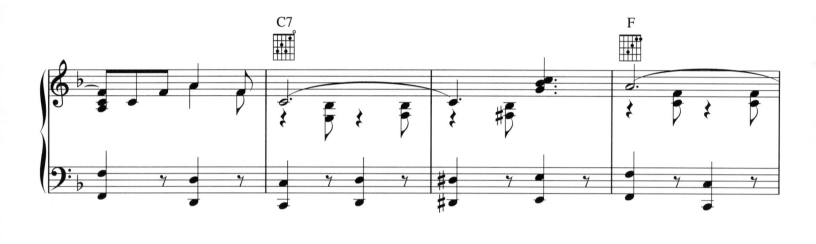

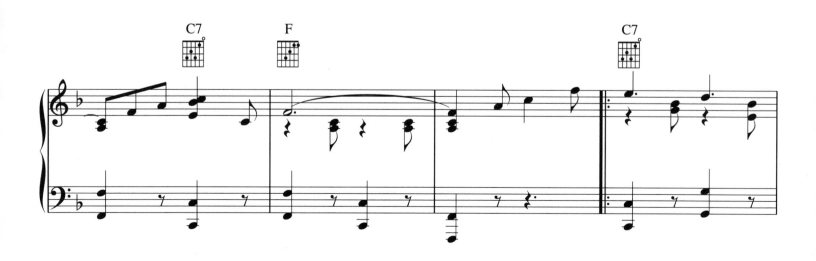

STARS AND STRIPES FOREVER

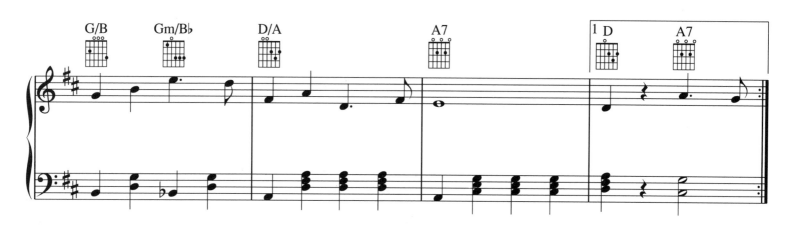

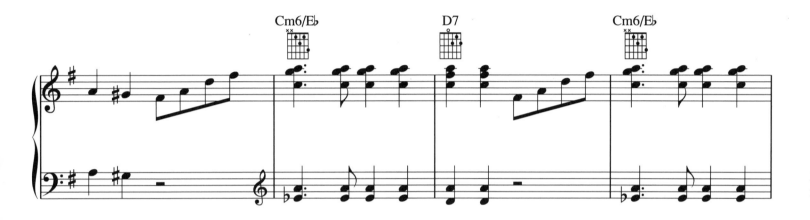

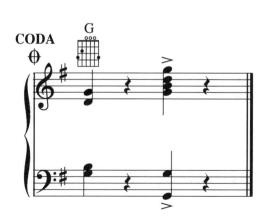

TRAMP, TRAMP, TRAMP

WASHINGTON POST MARCH

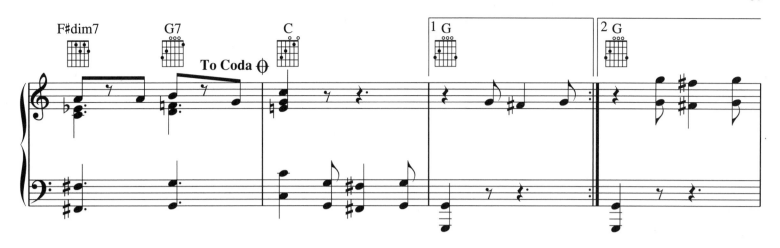

YANKEE DOODLE

WE ARE WITH YOU

Words and Music by
MICHAEL STEIN